EYEWITNESS PROJECT BOOKS
MEDIEVAL LIFE

by Susan Nicholson

LONDON, NEW YORK,
MELBOURNE, MUNICH, AND DELHI

Editorial Consultant Christopher Gravett
Educational Consultants Linda B. Gambrell
and Geraldine Taylor

Senior Editor Rob Houston
Assistant Editor Lisa Stock
Senior Art Editor Sarah Ponder
Managing Editor Camilla Hallinan
Managing Art Editor Owen Peyton Jones
DK Picture Library Claire Bowers, Lucy Claxton,
Rose Horridge, Emma Shephard
Picture Researcher Louise Thomas
Production Editor Hitesh Patel
Senior Production Controller Man Fai Lau
Jacket Designer Andy Smith
Art Director Martin Wilson

Designed for Dorling Kindersley by
Sands Publishing Solutions

First published in the United States in 2008 as
Eyewitness Workbooks Medieval Life
This edition published in Great Britain in 2009 by
Dorling Kindersley Limited,
80 Strand, London WC2R 0RL

A CIP catalogue record for this book
is available from the British Library.

ISBN: 978-1-40533-495-2

Colour reproduction by Colourscan, Singapore
Printed and bound by L.Rex Printing Co. Ltd, China

Discover more at
www.dk.com

Contents

Fast facts

How this book can help your child

Eyewitness Project Books offer a fun and colourful range of stimulating titles on the subjects of history, science, and geography. Specially designed to appeal to children of 8 years and up, each project book aims to:

- develop a child's knowledge of a popular topic
- provide practice of key skills and reinforce classroom learning
- nurture a child's special interest in a subject

The series is devised and written with the expert advice of educational and reading consultants, and supports the school curriculum.

About this book

Eyewitness Project Book Medieval Life is an activity-packed exploration of life in the Middle Ages. Inside you will find:

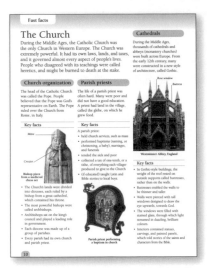

Fast facts

This section presents key information as concise facts that are easy to digest, learn, and remember. Encourage your child to start by reading through the valuable information in the Fast facts section and studying the statistics chart inside the flap at the back of the book before trying out the activities.

Activities

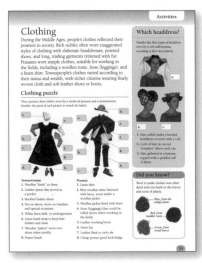

The enjoyable, fill-in activities are designed to develop information recall and help your child practise cross-referencing skills. Each activity can be completed using information provided on the page, in the Fast facts section, or on the back-cover flap. Your child should work systematically through the book and tackle just one or two activity topics per session. Encourage your child by checking answers together and offering extra guidance when necessary.

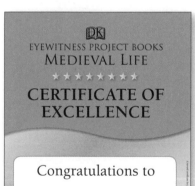

Quick quiz

There are six pages of multiple-choice questions to test your child's new-found knowledge of the subject. Children should only try answering the quiz questions once all of the activity section has been completed. As your child finishes each page of themed questions, check the answers together.

Answers and Progress Chart

All the answers are supplied in full at the back of the book, so no prior knowledge of the subject is required.

Use the Progress chart to motivate your child, and be positive about his or her achievements. On the completion of each activity or quiz topic, reward good work with a gold star.

PROGRESS CHART

Chart your progress as you work through the activity and quiz pages in this book. First check your answers, then stick a gold star in the correct box below.

Page	Topic	Star	Page	Topic	Star	Page	Topic	Star
14	Medieval timeline	★	24	A soldier's life	★	34	Medieval cathedrals	★
15	Medieval timeline	★	25	Living on a manor	★	35	Living in a monastery	★
16	Medieval remains	★	26	A peasant's lot	★	36	The written word	★
17	A feudal society	★	27	Town life	★	37	Disease and death	★
18	Castle life	★	28	Trade across Europe	★	38	History of the Middle Ages	★
19	Castle life	★	29	Clothing	★	39	Medieval society	★
20	Court and kings	★	30	Food and drink	★	40	Medieval warriors	★
21	Medieval knights	★	31	A medieval feast	★	41	Daily life	★
22	Training for battle	★	32	Fun and games	★	42	Guilds and trades	★
23	Heraldry for battle	★	33	Music and dancing	★	43	The medieval Church	★

Certificate

There is a Certificate of excellence at the back of the book for your child to fill in, remove, and display on the wall.

Lift the flap

The chart inside the back-cover flap is a fun learning tool, packed with fascinating facts and figures about medieval life. Happy learning!

Important information

• Please supervise your child for the cooking activity of page 31. Also make sure that your child takes care with scissors or a craft knife when making the "Fox and Geese" game on page 32 and in the "Design a window" activity on page 34. All other activities can be done without adult supervision.

• Encourage your child's interest with further research online and at your local library. Find out if your local museum has medieval exhibits, or if there are any medieval sites or monuments in your area. Some castles organize events such as jousts and fairs that bring history vividly to life.

The medieval world

The word "medieval" comes from the words *medium aevum*, which are Latin for "middle ages". The Middle Ages cover the period roughly between the fall of the western Roman Empire in the 5th century and the Renaissance – a rebirth in learning at the end of the 15th century.

The Dark Ages

The early part of the Middle Ages, from around 400 to 800 CE, is known as the "Dark" Ages. At the beginning of this period, Germanic tribes pushed across the frontiers of the western Roman Empire, destroying towns and making trade routes dangerous. The Dark Ages describes the centuries of disorder that followed.

Key facts

- In 476 CE, the last emperor of Rome lost his throne.
- The Saxons settled in Britain, the Franks took over Gaul (France), and the Goths invaded Italy.
- From the 700s, Vikings from the Scandinavian countries of Norway, Sweden, and Denmark began to raid the coasts of Europe.
- Art and learning survived in remote monasteries.

Viking warrior's helmet

New kingdoms

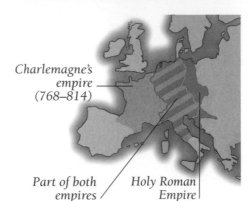

Charlemagne's empire (768–814)

Part of both empires / *Holy Roman Empire*

Part of Charlemagne's empire later became the Holy Roman Empire

Gradually, new kingdoms ruled by strong leaders began to emerge, and life in Europe became more stable. This encouraged trade and the growth of towns and cities, and the population of Europe rose.

Key facts

- In the 8th century, a great Frankish leader called Charles the Great, or Charlemagne (742–814), united an empire covering much of modern France and Germany.
- The lands of the Franks gradually became France, ruled by a king.
- Alfred the Great (846–899) defeated the Vikings to become king in southern England.
- Otto I (912–973) united the German states and was crowned Roman Emperor by the pope.

Medieval kings

Most medieval kings believed they had absolute power over their subjects, given to them by God. The king's royal court was the centre and showpiece of the kingdom, where the king demonstrated his power with great ceremonies and banquets.

Key facts

- Kingdoms were divided into many smaller states, or duchies, each ruled by powerful nobles called barons.
- Kings had to work hard to control their barons so that the barons did not become too powerful.
- To rebel against the king was almost like defying God. But if a king was weak or poor, his barons might try to take away his power.
- Kings often lured their noblemen to court, where they could keep an eye on them.

Medieval king

- Court entertainment included mock battles or tourneys, in which large groups of armoured knights charged at each other on horseback.
- Another attraction was the joust, a contest of fighting skills between two knights who each tried to unhorse the other with a lance.
- Medieval courts also had minstrels, who sang songs about love and brave deeds.

Medieval society

Throughout most of medieval Europe, society was organized into a feudal system, which stretched from the top to the bottom of society. In the feudal system, land was awarded to people in return for their services. At the top was the king. At the bottom were the peasants, who worked on the land.

Medieval women

Spindle

Peasant woman feeding chickens

The medieval Church taught that women were inferior to men, and should be meek and obedient to their fathers and husbands. When a woman married, she had to give any lands she owned to her husband. Even though medieval women had few rights, many worked for a living.

The feudal system

In the feudal system, the king gave land, or fiefs, to the barons and bishops. The barons became the king's servants, or vassals. They promised to serve the king and provide him with soldiers in times of war.

Mounted knight of the 1300s

Key facts

- Some powerful barons governed their fiefs as independent states, with their own private armies.
- Each baron divided his lands between lower lords, or knights, who became the baron's vassals, bound by oath to serve him.
- By around 1000, many vassals in England paid a tax called "scutage" (shield money) instead of fighting for the king.
- Peasants had no vassals and very few rights.

Crime & punishment

In medieval society, punishment for crimes was usually harsh. Convicted criminals might be dragged behind a horse, whipped, or hanged, depending on the nature of their crime.

Key facts

- Peasants who broke the law were tried by their lord in their lord's court. Their lord had almost complete power over them.
- Sometimes, people were locked in the stocks (a wooden frame with holes for the prisoner's ankles), or a pillory (which held a prisoner's neck and wrists in the same way).
- Lords and barons sometimes had to pay their king large sums of money to make sure that they got a fair trial.

A public hanging

Key facts

- Peasant women toiled in the fields, along with their husbands.
- The wives and daughters of craftsmen were often employed in workshops. Some even operated as tradeswomen in their own right.
- Wealthy ladies often organized large households. Some ran their estates when their husbands died or were away at war or at court, settling local disputes, managing farmlands, and handling finances.
- Spinning was almost always done by women. Many single women, especially, earned their living in this way (resulting in the term "spinster" for an unmarried woman).

Wool twists into thread as spindle twirls

Hand-held spindle

The age of castles

A castle was the fortified residence of a king or a baron, built to keep its occupants safe from enemy attack. Although a castle was a stronghold, with towering walls, watchtowers, and heavily fortified doors, it was also an administrative centre and a home, and its occupants could live there in comfort and style.

Castle development

The earliest castles appeared in the 9th and 10th centuries, in areas now part of France, Germany, and northern Italy. Most were earth ramparts, or walls, surrounded by a ditch and a timber fence.

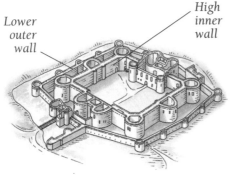

Lower outer wall

High inner wall

Concentric castle

Key facts

- Motte and bailey castles were built in the 11th and 12th centuries.
- The motte was an earth mound, topped by a wooden tower. The bailey was a courtyard, surrounded by a ditch and a timber fence.
- By the 11th century, some towers (called donjons, or keeps) were built of stone.
- In the 13th century, the keep was usually surrounded by a stone "curtain wall".
- From the mid-13th century, people built concentric castles, with rings of stone walls, one inside the other.

Castle people

The household of a large castle could easily contain as many people as a village. As well as the lord and his family, there were officials, soldiers, and a host of servants and craftsmen.

Key facts

- The lord's second-in-command was called the constable.
- Domestic servants included the cook, scullions (who helped prepare the meals), laundresses, and spinsters (who spun wool).
- Outdoor servants included dog-keepers, gardeners, and grooms.
- The castle's garrison was made up of knights and hired soldiers.
- Skilled craftsmen included carpenters, blacksmiths, and armourers.

Lord   **Lady**

Attack and defence

Castles were built to be defended, with strong walls and doors. They also needed plenty of storage space for food and a deep well for water, to withstand a long siege if surrounded by enemy soldiers.

Key facts

Castle attackers could:

- shoot arrows
- hurl missiles over the walls with trebuchets and other catapults
- scale walls with ladders
- break down walls and doors with battering rams
- try to undermine walls by tunnelling beneath them
- wait until the inhabitants starved.

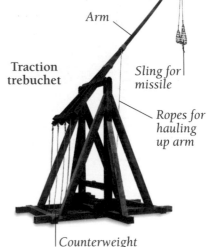

Arm

Traction trebuchet

Sling for missile

Ropes for hauling up arm

Counterweight

Castle defenders could:

- shoot arrows
- hurl missiles over the walls with catapults
- push away scaling ladders with forked poles
- lower hooks to catch the heads of battering rams
- dig countermines to break into tunnels
- ration supplies to make them last.

Running a manor

During the Middle Ages, more than ninety per cent of the population lived and worked on manors. Manors usually consisted of the lord's house or castle, a village, a church, and the surrounding countryside. The lord and lady of the manor oversaw the running of the estate and the household, but they also had plenty of free time for leisure activities, such as hunting and hawking.

The peasants

The peasants, also known as serfs or villeins, lived in the village. The peasants worked for their lord, who let them farm a piece of land for themselves in return for their labour on the manor.

Key facts

- Serfs – along with their land, animals, homes, food, and clothes – belonged to their lord and could not leave the manor without permission.
- A serf could become free only by saving enough money to buy a plot of land, or by marrying a free person.
- Life was hard – many peasants lived no longer than 25 years.

Windowless walls

Straw roof

Single door

Peasant's house

Manor officials

The lord appointed officials to help him run the manor. The most important was the steward, who was a well-paid, powerful figure in the district. His second-in-command was the bailiff.

The steward or a treasurer looked after the lord's money

The lord settled disputes and judged crimes

Written records might be kept of the lord's decisions

Key facts

- The steward organized the farm work, kept accounts of the manor's money, and acted as a judge at the manor court if the lord was away.
- The bailiff allotted jobs to the peasants and hired skilled craftsmen to repair buildings and tools.
- The bailiff was assisted by the reeve – a peasant chosen by the other villagers.

Manor life

Without machines, all farm work was done by hand, using simple tools. Crops were grown around the village in two or three big fields. Peasants were allotted some land in each field, so the good and bad soil was shared out equally between them.

Peasants pushing a hay cart up a slope

Key facts

- The peasants hoed and harvested their own plots, or strips, of land, but worked together on large jobs such as ploughing and hay-making.
- If the harvest was poor, the whole village starved.
- Most manors had one water mill, owned by the lord, used to grind grain into flour.
- The peasants had to give some of their grain to the lord in exchange for using the mill.
- On some manors, villagers might also have to pay to bake bread in the lord's oven, and use his wine press for their grapes.
- Every autumn, the lord allowed his serfs to let their pigs feed on nuts in his private wood, in a custom called pannage.

Peasant with his pig in his lord's woods

The Church

During the Middle Ages, the Catholic Church was the only Church in Western Europe. The Church was extremely powerful. It had its own laws, lands, and taxes, and it governed almost every aspect of people's lives. People who disagreed with its teachings were called heretics, and might be burned to death at the stake.

Church organization

The head of the Catholic Church was called the Pope. People believed that the Pope was God's representative on Earth. The Pope ruled over the Church from Rome, in Italy.

Key facts

Mitre

Crozier

Bishop piece from a medieval chess set

- The Church's lands were divided into dioceses, each ruled by a bishop from a great cathedral, which contained his throne.
- The most powerful bishops were called archbishops.
- Archbishops sat on the king's council and played a leading role in government.
- Each diocese was made up of a group of parishes.
- Every parish had its own church and parish priest.

Parish priests

The life of a parish priest was often hard. Many were poor and did not have a good education. A priest had land in the village, called the glebe, on which he grew food.

Key facts

A parish priest:

- held church services, such as mass
- performed baptisms (naming, or christening, a baby), marriages, and funerals
- tended the sick and poor
- collected a tax of one-tenth, or a tithe, of everything each villager produced to give to the Church
- (if educated) taught Latin and Bible stories to local boys.

Parish priest performing a baptism in church

Cathedrals

During the Middle Ages, thousands of cathedrals and abbeys (monastery churches) were built across Europe. From the early 12th century, many were constructed in a new style of architecture, called Gothic.

Rose window

Buttress

Westminster Abbey, England

Key facts

- In Gothic-style buildings, the weight of the roof rested on outside supports called buttresses, rather than on the walls.
- Buttresses enabled the walls to be thinner and taller.
- Walls were pierced with tall windows designed to draw the eye upwards, towards God.
- The windows were filled with stained glass, through which light streamed in dazzling, brilliant colours.
- Interiors contained statues, carvings, and painted panels, which told stories of the saints and characters from the Bible.

Monastic life

During the Middle Ages, many people chose to live a religious life, as a monk in a monastery or as a nun in a convent. Monasteries and convents were self-contained worlds, separate from the rest of society. Each was ruled by an abbot or an abbess, and the monks and nuns followed special rules.

Monastic orders

The first monastic order was founded by St Benedict in the 6th century, in Monte Cassino, Italy. The monks became known as the Benedictines because they followed the Rule of St Benedict.

Key facts

- The Rule of St Benedict instructed monks to make three vows – of poverty (to own no property), chastity (never to marry), and obedience (to obey the orders of their leaders).
- In time, monasteries and convents throughout Europe adopted the Rule of St Benedict.
- Other monastic orders included the Cluniacs, Carthusians, Cistercians, and Franciscans.

St Benedict

Scholarship

Many monks were well educated and some monasteries became centres of great learning, with libraries filled with books. Monks spent much time in the scriptorium copying out prayers, psalms, or the Bible.

Monk at work in the scriptorium

Key facts

- A long manuscript, such as the Bible, might take one scribe a year to copy out by hand.
- Many manuscripts were beautifully decorated, or illuminated, with jewel-like paints and precious gold leaf as a way of glorifying God.
- Because they were made by hand, books remained scarce until the development of printing in the 1450s.

Daily life

A monk's or nun's day was spent attending a cycle of eight regular church services. In traditional Benedictine monasteries, these began with Matins at dawn and ended with Compline at nightfall. In addition to time spent at private prayer and meditation, there were also many jobs to do around the monastery or convent.

Monks at prayer

Key facts

- The cycle of services or offices in a traditional Benedictine monastery included Matins (dawn), Prime (6am), Terce (9am), Sext (noon), Nones, (3pm), Vespers (6pm, or dusk), and Compline (9pm or nightfall).
- Daily jobs included washing and cooking; growing vegetables and grain; bee-keeping; and making wine and ale.
- Monks also copied out religious texts, looked after the sick, and educated boys and novices (trainee monks).
- Monks were named according to their jobs. For example, the almoner gave out alms (food and money) to the poor and sick.

Medieval towns

Some medieval towns grew up around a castle, where people hoped to be safe from attack. Some developed around trading centres, such as a busy crossroads or a village where local farmers gathered to sell their produce. Others grew up near natural harbours and big rivers, where it was easy to bring in goods by ship.

Medieval walled town

The town charter

At first, towns were parts of a king's or a lord's domain. As they became richer, townspeople resented having to work on the lord's land. Instead, townspeople paid their lord a fixed yearly sum in return for a charter, which gave them the right to govern themselves.

Key facts

- A charter made a town a free borough, with the power to hold a market, make its own laws, form guilds, and raise taxes.
- The townspeople became free citizens, or burgesses.
- The towns were governed by an elected mayor and a local council.
- Any peasants who had run away to live in a town became free men if they avoided capture for a year.

Town walls

Most medieval towns were fortified with high stone walls and strong gatehouses. This kept out enemies and also made sure that merchants and other visitors could only enter by the gates, where they had to pay a toll.

Key facts

- Town gates were opened at dawn and locked at dusk.
- At sunset, the town bells rang to sound the curfew, telling everyone to finish work and lock their doors.
- Curfew was also the signal for people to cover their fires with dome-shaped clay pots before they went to bed.
- As the dark streets could be unsafe, nightwatchmen patrolled them with lanterns to deter criminals.

Nightwatchman's lantern

Town houses

As space inside a town's walls was limited, houses were built close together. Upper storeys often jutted out above lower floors, making streets dark and gloomy.

Medieval home and shop

Key facts

- Although houses did not have bathrooms or running water, most towns had public bathhouses, and some people bathed twice a day.
- As there were no drains or sewers, people emptied slop pails and chamber pots out of windows onto the street below.
- Most craftsmen had workshops on the ground floor of their home.
- Goods were displayed on a hinged shelf at the front. Shutters were pulled down for security at night.
- As few people could read, shops hung out a symbol of their trade, such as a loaf of bread for a baker.
- The same type of traders or craftsmen often had shops on the same street. In London, for example, tailors worked on Threadneedle Street.

Trade and guilds

The first medieval merchants were pedlars who wandered from village to village, selling goods. By the 12th century, Europe had grown more prosperous and more goods were produced. Merchants became dealers, employers, and shipowners, who transported goods along a huge network of trade routes that linked the main European towns.

Money matters

Merchants had to keep careful accounts of their money. Early traders kept their money in strong money boxes. Later, traders used bills of exchange (as a kind of cheque) instead of carrying large sums of money.

Key facts

- Most coins were silver but, in 1252, the city of Florence in Italy minted the first gold coins since Roman times – the golden florin.
- Many medieval merchants carried small coin balances to weigh different coins and currencies and check their value.
- Banking began in Italy with moneylenders who did business on benches, or "banks". Bankers grew rich through the interest they charged for their services.

Medieval merchant weighing coins

Fairs and markets

Merchants traded many goods throughout Europe and the Middle East, from finely woven cloth, to metalwork, spices, jewels, coal, and even goose feathers (used for stuffing mattresses).

Medieval market trader

Key facts

- International trade was mainly done at great fairs, which took place once or twice a year and lasted up to two weeks.
- One of the most famous fairs was held in Champagne, a province in eastern France.
- Rich families sent their stewards to the fairs, to buy provisions to last them through the winter.
- Local trade took place in markets held in towns and villages.
- Town markets were usually held two or three times a week.

Guilds

Guilds were associations of craftspeople, formed to control the craft's business for its members. In 1261, a book of trades listed around 100 crafts in Paris, each with its own guild. By the 1420s, guilds existed in most big European towns.

Hat

Fur trim

Expensive leather boots

Belt-bag for money

Clothing worn by a guild master

Key facts

- Guilds had strict rules about their trade, such as how long guild members could work and how much they must charge.
- Guild members who did not maintain high standards of workmanship were fined, or expelled from the guild.
- Some wealthy guilds started schools, or arranged entertainment for the townspeople on holy days.
- Most guilds supported poorer members, providing them with money from a central fund.
- Women were not usually allowed to become guild members.
- Rich guilds had chambers, or guildhalls, where members met for banquets or to settle disputes.

Medieval timeline

The Middle Ages can be divided into three periods. The "Dark" Ages describes the centuries of disorder lasting from around 400, after the fall of the Roman Empire, to 1000. The period from 1000 to 1300 is often called the High Middle Ages. During this time, life in Europe became more settled. Many great castles and cathedrals were built, and the Catholic Church reached the height of its power. The Late Middle Ages, from 1300 to 1500, was a time of change. In the 1300s, famine and plague killed one-third of the population of Europe, and France and England were often at war. In the 1400s, there was a rebirth, or renaissance, of interest in art and science.

Finish the timeline

Fill in the missing dates in the timeline, which charts important events during the Middle Ages. Choose from the dates below, using the information on page 6 and the back-cover chart to help you. Then find four stickers to match the events.

962	476
1066	c. 1385
c. 1267	768
1346	1210
1415	1492

....
The last emperor of the Roman Empire in the West loses power. (The Roman Empire in the East – called the Byzantine Empire – continues until 1453).

c. 500
Benedict founds the Benedictine order of monks.

527
Justinian I becomes eastern Roman Emperor. Byzantine culture flourishes.

Francis of Assisi

570
Mohammed, the prophet of Islam, is born at Mecca in Arabia.

c. 750
Epic poem *Beowulf*, the adventures of a Scandinavian warrior, is written in Old English.

731
The monk Bede completes his *Ecclesiastical History of the English People*.

King John sealing the Magna Carta

1144
Romanesque church of St Denis in France is rebuilt in the Gothic style.

c. 1200
First university is established in Perugia, Italy.

....
Francis of Assisi founds the Franciscan order of friars.

1215
English barons force King John of England to accept the Magna Carta, which limits the powers of the king.

c. 1248
Theologian Thomas Aquinas teaches at the University of Paris.

1266
Italian explorer Marco Polo reaches the court of Kublai Khan in China.

The Black Death kills one-third of Europe's population

Gutenberg's Bible, printed *c.* 1455

1347
The Black Death, a deadly plague, sweeps across Europe.

1358
Boccaccio completes his great work, *The Decameron.*

1381
English peasants, led by Wat Tyler, revolt against high taxes.

....
Geoffrey Chaucer starts to write *The Canterbury Tales.*

....
The English defeat the French at the Battle of Agincourt.

c. 1439
Johannes Gutenberg invents moveable type.

Colour the map

Colour in the area ruled by Charlemagne when his empire was at its height, using the map on page 6 to help you.

When Charlemagne died, his empire was broken up. Some of his lands later became part of the empire of Otto I. Otto's successors added to these territories and came to rule a huge area which became known as the Holy Roman Empire.

Still using the map on page 6 as a guide, draw an outline to show the borders of the Holy Roman Empire.

Charlemagne

Cross mark of William of Normandy

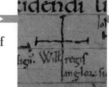

Crusaders

....	**871**	....	....	**1086**	**1095**
Charlemagne becomes ruler of the Franks.	Alfred becomes king of Wessex in England.	Otto I, or Otto the Great, is crowned Roman Emperor by the pope.	William of Normandy defeats English king Harold at the Battle of Hastings.	Domesday Book – a survey of land and resources in England – is compiled.	The crusades begin against the Muslims of the Middle East.

....	**1297**	**1307**	**1315**	**1337**	....
Giotto, founder of the modern style of painting, is born in Florence.	French King Louis IX is made into a saint by the Church.	Italian poet Dante begins his famous poem *The Divine Comedy*.	Bad weather and crop failure leads to widespread famine in Europe.	Beginning of the Hundred Years' War – a series of battles between France and England.	English defeat the French at the Battle of Crécy.

Byzantine mosaic

Coin depicting Tudor king Henry VII

1452	**1453**	**1485**	....
Renaissance artist Leonardo da Vinci is born in Florence, Italy.	Constantinople is captured by Ottoman Turks. End of Byzantine civilization.	The Tudor dynasty begins in England, with the reign of Henry VII.	Christopher Columbus crosses the Atlantic, claiming America for the Spanish.

Did you know?

The Domesday Book was commissioned by William the Conqueror to find out how much money he could raise in taxes.

Medieval remains

Even though the Middle Ages ended over 500 years ago, many of the artefacts or objects used by people in their daily lives have survived. These, together with written records and the remains of buildings, such as homes, workshops, and churches, help us understand how people lived during medieval times.

Medieval covered market in Aquitaine, France

Name it!

Identify these medieval objects from their descriptions given in the artefact fact box on the right.

1. ....

2. ....

3. ....
....

4. ....
....

5. ....

6. ....

Everyday things

Find stickers of three everyday objects used in a medieval home.

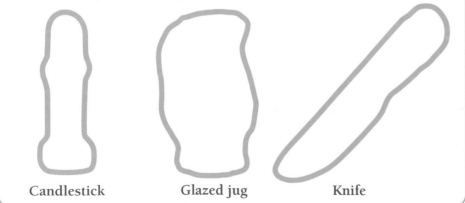

Candlestick   **Glazed jug**   **Knife**

Artefact facts

- People used a pottery **chamber pot** at night, rather than visiting an outside toilet.

- Wealthy people sometimes tiled the floors of their homes. This **floor tile** shows a picture of a castle surrounded by four fleurs de lys.

- A musical instrument called a **psaltery** was played by plucking its strings with goose quills.

- People wore accessories with their clothes, such as a hair pin, a brooch, or a decorative **belt buckle.**

- Books, like this **folding book**, were usually handwritten on parchment, a kind of thick paper made from animal skin.

- A **calendar stave** was a stick carved to keep a record of the passing days and months.

Did you know?

This sheep's horn was used to store tooth powder for cleaning teeth. The powder was ground from cuttlefish and oyster shells.

A feudal society

The feudal system was used in France by the Normans from around 900. After William of Normandy conquered England in 1066, the system was introduced there, too. The feudal system became an established way of life throughout much of Europe for over 300 years.

Duke William of Normandy, also known as William the Conqueror

Did you know?

When a noble swore an oath of loyalty to be the king's servant, or vassal, he knelt before the king and spoke the words, "Sire, I become your man."

Feudal word puzzle

Draw a line from each word to its correct meaning. Use the information on pages 7 and 9 to help you.

1. Scutage	a. A system in which the peasants were allowed to feed their pigs in their lord's woods.
2. Vassal	b. "Shield money" paid to a king or baron to hire soldiers instead of fighting for him.
3. Fief	c. Land granted to a noble or lord in exchange for loyalty and services.
4. Pannage	d. A servant, sworn to serve a noble or king.

Who's who in the feudal system

Find stickers to illustrate this account of the feudal system. Then fill in the missing words from the list below, using the information on pages 6 and 7 to help you.

knights	king	barons
nobles	peasants	bishops

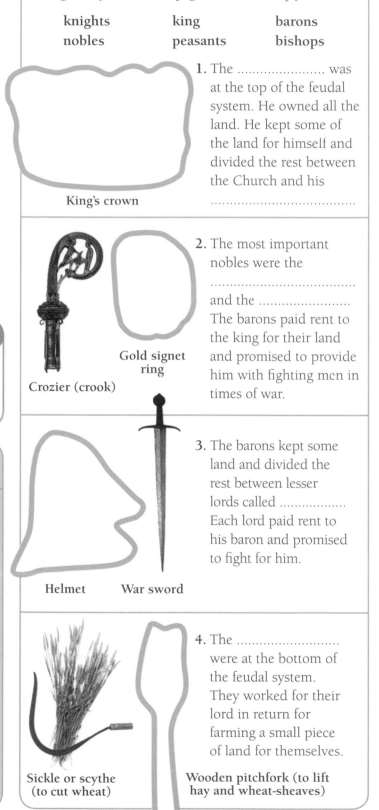

King's crown

1. The .... was at the top of the feudal system. He owned all the land. He kept some of the land for himself and divided the rest between the Church and his ....

Crozier (crook)

Gold signet ring

2. The most important nobles were the .... and the .... The barons paid rent to the king for their land and promised to provide him with fighting men in times of war.

Helmet   War sword

3. The barons kept some land and divided the rest between lesser lords called .... Each lord paid rent to his baron and promised to fight for him.

Sickle or scythe (to cut wheat)   Wooden pitchfork (to lift hay and wheat-sheaves)

4. The .... were at the bottom of the feudal system. They worked for their lord in return for farming a small piece of land for themselves.

Castle life

From the ninth century onwards, medieval kings and lords lived in castles. Early castles were often cold and draughty because the only heating came from open fires in large, stone rooms. Everyone usually slept in the castle's main room, the Great Hall. By the 13th century, most people slept where they worked, but the lord's family and important inhabitants, such as the castle's chaplain or priest, had their own rooms.

Castle facts

1. The moat, a water-filled trench surrounding the castle, made it difficult for attackers to approach the castle walls, or dig a tunnel beneath them.

2. A hinged drawbridge across the moat could be raised in seconds.

3. The castle's guardroom was at the top of the tower above the drawbridge.

4. Soldiers patrolled the battlements on a wall-walk, a path that ran along the top of the walls.

5. Prisoners were sometimes kept in an underground cell, called a dungeon.

6. The fire at the forge in the central courtyard was used to heat iron to make horseshoes, tools, armour, and weapons.

7. A deep well supplied the castle's inhabitants with fresh water.

8. The lord's bedroom was in the keep – the largest and strongest tower.

9. Feasts were held in the Great Hall, a large richly decorated room in the keep.

10. The chapel, which was above the Great Hall, had a row of tall stained-glass windows.

11. Food was prepared in the castle kitchen in a huge wood-fired oven or over an open fire.

12. Huge stone tanks called cisterns stored rainwater for use in the kitchen.

13. Storerooms were filled with sacks of grain and barrels of salted meat and beer.

14. Cesspits for toilet waste were cleaned out regularly by servants called gong farmers.

Castle quiz

This picture shows a cross-section of a 14th-century French castle. Read the descriptions of different parts of the castle, then find and number the same parts in the picture.

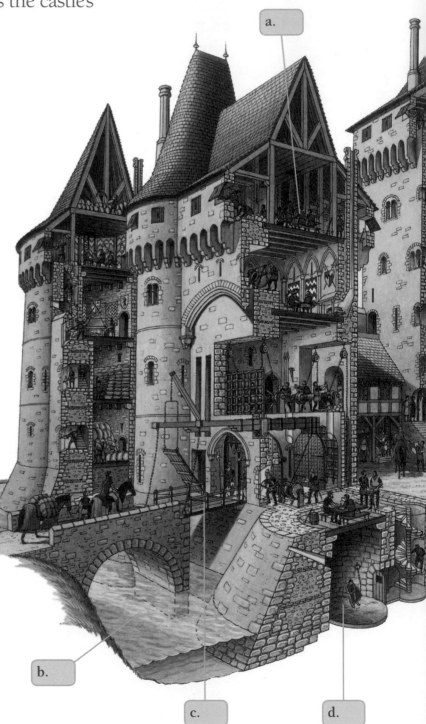

Building a castle

A massive stone castle took many years to build and a huge workforce, including masons (stoneworkers), carpenters (woodworkers), smiths (metalworkers), and plumbers. Draw a line to match each worker to the job description.

1. Master mason
2. Rough mason
3. Carpenter
4. Quarry worker
5. Plumber
6. Smith

a. Made wooden joists, floors, and roofs.
b. Cut stone from the ground in quarries.
c. Took charge of all the building work.
d. Piped water and sewage.
e. Forged metal hinges, chains, and tools.
f. Smoothed rough blocks of stone.

Stonemasons
at work

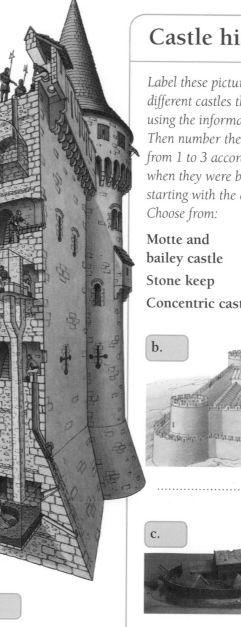

Castle history

Label these pictures of three different castles through the ages, using the information on page 8. Then number the pictures from 1 to 3 according to when they were built, starting with the earliest. Choose from:

**Motte and
bailey castle**

Stone keep

Concentric castle

a.

....

....

b.

....

c.

....

Court and kings

Medieval kings ruled their lands from the royal court – a magnificent castle designed to impress their subjects. Most kings governed through a council of churchmen and barons. In England, this was called the Great Council. At court, the king set taxes, settled disputes, and made laws. In 1264, English baron Simon de Montfort led a rebellion to limit the power of the king, Henry III. He called the first-ever English "parliament" made up of the old Council plus representatives from every shire (district) and town.

12th-century chess piece of a medieval king

Mix-and-match kings

Draw lines to match each king to the correct description. Use the information on the back-cover chart to help you.

1. French king made into a saint for his goodness and religious beliefs
2. First Norman king of England who invaded the country in 1066
3. King of Wessex who fought the Vikings
4. Famous early king of the Franks
5. English king who defeated the French in 1415
6. German king, crowned Roman Emperor in 962 by the Pope

a. Charlemagne

b. William I (the Conqueror)

c. Louis IX

d. Alfred the Great

e. Otto I

f. Henry V

Chivalry facts

- The word "chivalry" comes from the French word *cheval*, for horse, because knights rode on horseback.

- Chivalry describes a code of behaviour followed by knights, which emphasized respect and good manners towards women.

- In the 12th century, a kind of romance called courtly love, became fashionable.

- Courtly love had strict rules. It had to be secret, and the knight had to promise to do brave deeds for his love.

Find a sticker of a 15th-century Flemish shield showing courtly love.

King and court life quiz

Use the information on this page and page 6 to answer the following questions.

1. Name two ways in which kings kept the barons entertained at court.

....
....

2. What was the code of behaviour followed by knights, which stressed good manners towards women?

....

3. What French word does "chivalry" come from?

....

4. Name the romance that became fashionable in the 12th century.

....

Medieval knights

The knights were the warriors of the medieval world, who fought on horseback with lances and swords. A knight was usually born into a noble family and was trained from boyhood to use weapons, wear armour, and ride a heavy war horse called a destrier.

Arming a knight

These pictures and captions show six stages of a knight being armed by his squire. Number the stages 1 to 6 to put them in the right order.

Mail skirt

a.

The squire ties a mail skirt around the knight's waist and buckles on his leg armour.

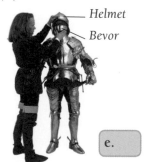

Gauntlet

b.

The gauntlets are fitted with leather gloves, so the knight can easily grip his sword.

Backplate

Waist strap

c.

The back- and breastplate (called the cuirass) are joined together by straps.

Arming doublet

d.

First, the knight puts on the arming doublet, a garment onto which his armour is tied.

Helmet

Bevor

e.

A chin defence, called a bevor, is fitted, followed by a type of helmet called a sallet.

f.

The elbow defence, or couter, is laced on between the upper and lower arm defences.

Did you know?

A suit of plate armour weighed 25 kg (55 lb) – about the same as a seven-year-old child.

Knight facts

- At the age of about seven, a boy of noble birth was sent away to another nobleman's household to become a page.
- A page learned courtly manners, horse riding, and how to fight.
- When about 14, a page became a squire, apprenticed to a particular knight.
- The word squire comes from the French word *ecuyer*, meaning shield-bearer.
- A squire was trained to use weapons. He also had to look after his master's armour and horses, help him if he was hurt, and carve meat at the table.
- Successful squires were knighted when they were around 21 at a ceremony called dubbing.

Dubbing a knight

Making a knight

Fill in the missing words, using the information in the Knight facts box, then find a sticker of a page.

1. When he was about seven years old, a boy became a ....
2. At around 14, a page became a ....
3. A squire looked after the knight's .... and ....
4. A squire became a knight at the age of around ....

Page

Training for battle

By the 12th century, knights and other fighting men trained for battle in tournaments. Two teams of knights fought each other in a mock fight called a tourney or mêlée. During the 13th century a dramatic new element was added to the tournament – the joust, in which two knights charged at each other on horseback, each trying to unseat his opponent with a lance.

Did you know?

Knights often painted their lances so they were the same colour as their coat of arms.

Jousting facts

- A knight won the joust by unhorsing the other knight with a single blow of his lance.

- Points were scored if a knight broke his lance on his opponent's shield.

- If a lance was broken three times, the knights might then fight with swords on foot.

- In jousts of war, knights used sharp lances, which could kill their opponents.

- In jousts of peace, knights used lances fitted with a blunt tip or a coronel, which was shaped like a small crown.

- A barrier called the tilt was introduced in the 15th century, to separate the knights and avoid collisions.

Joust quiz

Use the information on this page to answer the following questions.

1. Why did knights take part in tournaments?

....

2. What were mock battles called?

....

3. In what type of joust did knights use sharp lances?

....

4. What was introduced in the 15th century to stop jousting knights riding into each other?

....

5. What was a coronel?

....

Jousting knight

Joust puzzle

Draw lines from the labels to the correct parts of this jousting scene.

Raised box for important spectators

Jousting knights

The list (area of land enclosed for jousting)

Knight on horseback waiting to take part in the joust

Banners, or flags, showing each knight's coat of arms

Cloth pavilions, or tents, for each knight, and his squire and weapons

Wounded knight lying outside his pavilion

Heraldry for battle

During the 12th century, the designs that knights used to decorate their shields became standardized in a system called heraldry. This meant that every knight could be identified by the symbols on his shield, called his coat of arms. Heraldry was based on strict rules. Each coat of arms used a combination of standard colours and "metals" (silver or gold), and was described in a special language, based on Old French.

Quartered design shows the arms of two families joined by marriage

A jar from around 1500, bearing a coat of arms

Match the shield

Look at the key then number each shield to match the descriptions.

1. Azure, a sun in splendour Or
2. Lozengy, Argent and gules
3. Or, a pale gules
4. Azure, a fess embattled Or
5. Sable, a cross engrailed Or
6. Gules, a lion rampant Or
7. Vert, a crescent Or
8. Or, a portcullis purpure

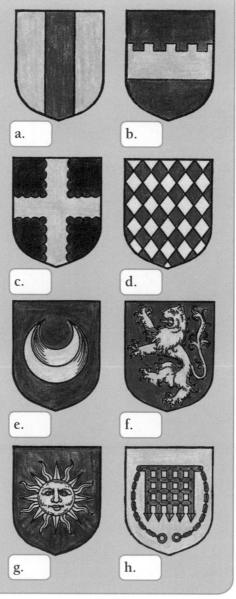

a.　b.

c.　d.

e.　f.

g.　h.

KEY	
Or	Gold
Argent	Silver
Gules	Red
Azure	Blue
Sable	Black
Vert	Green
Purpure	Purple
Pale	Vertical band
Fess	Horizontal band
Engrailed	With a pattern of half circles
Embattled	Topped with row of small squares, like battlements

Design a shield

Design your own coat of arms here.

Using the key, can you describe your coat of arms?

....

....

Find the coat of arms

Find a sticker of a shield with the design called Vert, a castle Argent.

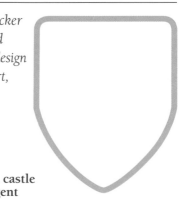

Vert, a castle Argent

A soldier's life

During the early Middle Ages, armoured knights were the most important fighting men. However, armies also included well-trained footsoldiers armed with spears, and archers skilled at using longbows. By the 15th century, knights had been largely replaced by professional, well-trained soldiers who fought with staff weapons (such as pollaxes and pikes) and, later, guns.

A medieval soldier's gear

Find six stickers to match these descriptions of a medieval soldier's armour and weapons.

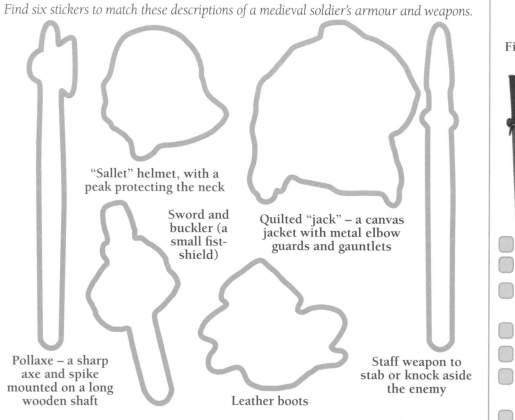

"Sallet" helmet, with a peak protecting the neck

Sword and buckler (a small fist-shield)

Quilted "jack" – a canvas jacket with metal elbow guards and gauntlets

Pollaxe – a sharp axe and spike mounted on a long wooden shaft

Leather boots

Staff weapon to stab or knock aside the enemy

Ready for war

Circle the correct word to complete the following sentences, using information on this page.

1. A medieval footsoldier's jacket was made of **sheepskin / canvas / silk**.
2. Metal parts on the jacket protected the soldier's **feet and knees / arms and hands / chest**.
3. The soldier's small shield was called a **gauntlet / sallet / buckler**.
4. The sallet protected the **elbow / head / shoulders**.
5. The pollaxe was a kind of **sword / shield / staff weapon**.

On the march

Medieval soldiers carried all their personal belongings in a canvas kit bag and belt-bag. Look at the pictures, then tick the two items that a soldier would NOT have carried with him.

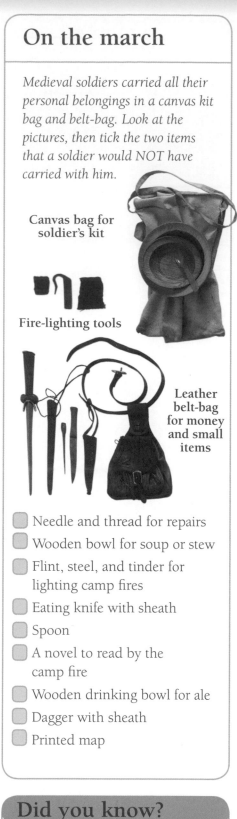

Canvas bag for soldier's kit

Fire-lighting tools

Leather belt-bag for money and small items

- Needle and thread for repairs
- Wooden bowl for soup or stew
- Flint, steel, and tinder for lighting camp fires
- Eating knife with sheath
- Spoon
- A novel to read by the camp fire
- Wooden drinking bowl for ale
- Dagger with sheath
- Printed map

Did you know?

The buckler was carried in the left hand. It was used to protect a soldier from blows and to hit his enemy in the face, before slashing or stabbing him with the sword.

Living on a manor

Most manors were isolated, far away from other villages. The villagers had to grow their own food and make everything else they needed, such as clothes and tools. The only visitors to the village were pilgrims on their way to a shrine, the occasional pedlar selling goods from a pack on his back, or soldiers. Most peasants never left the village in which they were born.

Falconry

A favourite sport of nobles was falconry – hunting wildfowl or other animals with a bird of prey.

Find a sticker of a peregrine falcon.

Jobs on the manor

Using the information on page 9, draw a line to match each person to his job.

1. Reeve
2. Steward
3. Lord
4. Peasant
5. Bailiff

a. Worked in the fields, growing crops.
b. Looked after the manor's money and organized the farmwork.
c. Told peasants and craftsmen what to do, and when.
d. Assisted the bailiff; made sure the peasants worked hard and did not steal.
e. Oversaw the running of the whole manor and its household.

Hunting puzzle

This picture shows a lord and lady of the manor at one of their favourite sports – hunting deer. Read the descriptions on the right, then find and fill in the labels.

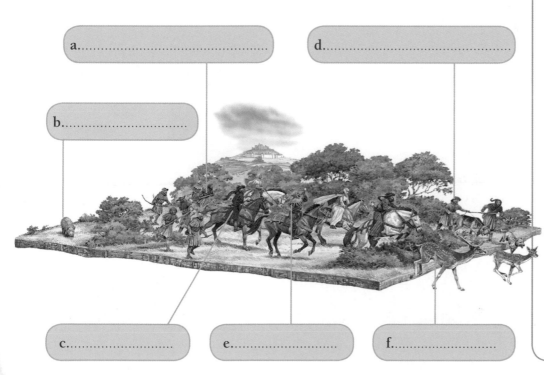

a.....................
b.....................
c.....................
d.....................
e.....................
f.....................

Hunting facts

- **Deer** provided the best hunting in the forest. After a deer was killed, it was eaten by the lord and his family.
- **Trackers** used bloodhounds to find the deer's scent, then scared the deer out of the undergrowth so the lord could give chase.
- The **lord** guarded his right to hunt in the forest. Anyone else caught poaching (hunting without permission) was severely punished.
- The **huntsman** sounded his horn to control the hunting dogs.
- **Servants** and villagers trailed the hunt on foot.
- **Wild boar** were also hunted in the forest.

A peasant's lot

Most peasants lived in simple one- or two-roomed cottages with straw roofs and walls made of woven strips of wood, covered with a mixture of animal dung, straw, and clay. Basic furniture might include a wooden table and bench, a chest for clothes, and a straw mattress. A fire lit in the stone hearth in the middle of one of the rooms would have provided warmth and heat for cooking but, as there was no chimney, would also have filled the room with smoke. The inside would also have been dark, as cottages did not usually have windows.

Statue of a medieval peasant, c. 1500

The farming year

Match the descriptions of the peasants' work to one of the four seasons in which it was done. Choose from:

spring summer autumn winter

1. In the coldest part of the year, peasants worked mainly indoors, repairing and making tools and clothes. If not too chilly, they also gathered firewood, pruned vines or fruit trees, and mended fences, hedges, and roofs.

   ....

2. In fine weather, peasants cut hay to use as animal feed through the autumn and winter. They also harvested grain crops such as wheat, threshed the wheat to loosen the grain from the ears, then ground the grain into flour to make bread.

   ....

3. After the cold weather passed, peasants ploughed the fields and scattered seeds by hand. They sheared sheep for their wool, and hoed and weeded the soil to look after the growing crops in the fields.

   ....

4. As the weather cooled, the peasants picked fruit to be dried or stored, and gathered nuts and berries. They also harvested grapes and pressed them to make wine. Pigs and cows were slaughtered and their meat smoked to last through the winter.

   ....

The grape harvest

How much tax?

Peasants had to give the local priest a tenth (or tithe) of everything they produced – from crops and firewood, to eggs and flour.

How much must this peasant give to the priest if he produced:

- 10 sacks of wheat grain   ....
- 30 bundles of firewood   ....
- 650 eggs   ....
- 1 barrel of ale   ....

Eggs

Sack of wheat

Firewood

Town life

Medieval towns were often mazes of twisting streets and lanes, full of shops where people could buy goods. As few people in medieval times could read, shopkeepers advertised their wares by hanging out a symbol of their trade, such as a loaf of bread for a baker. In some towns, people with the same trade or craft lived on the same street, so shoemakers worked in Shoe Lane, and cows were kept for milking on Milk Street.

Learning a trade

These captions give four stages in learning a trade. Number the stages 1 to 4 to put them in the correct order.

a. ☐ The new master craftsman opened his own shop and took on an apprentice to learn his trade.

b. ☐ At the age of 13 or 14, the apprentice became a journeyman, travelling from town to town and working for different master craftsmen to gain experience.

c. ☐ A child became an apprentice to a master craftsman between the ages of seven and nine, and served his apprenticeship for seven years.

d. ☐ To become a master, the journeyman joined a guild and presented other guild members with a "masterpiece" of his finest work.

An armourer and his apprentice

True or false?

Tick the boxes to show which of these statements are true or false. Use the information on this page and page 12 to help you.

	TRUE	FALSE
1. Many major medieval towns were governed by a lord mayor and a council of free citizens.	☐	☐
2. Most townhouses had bathrooms with flushing toilets and running water.	☐	☐
3. Craftspeople usually lived above their workshops.	☐	☐
4. Free citizens were called burgesses.	☐	☐
5. It was free to enter a medieval city.	☐	☐

Inside a townhouse

Look at the labels on the sticker sheet and find two items that might be found in a wealthy merchant's town house.

- Windows made of panes of polished horn
- A wooden bed with curtains, to keep out draughts
- A mattress stuffed with goose feathers
- A low table, stools, and benches
- A chair with a high back (for the head of the family)
- A large cooking pot
- A pewter goblet
- A spinning wheel, to spin wool into thread
- A tapestry, to hang on the wall
- Beeswax candles
- A privy (a closet in the wall with a hole over a cesspit)
- A chest for storing money or jewellery

Tapestry

Trade across Europe

By the 14th century, Europe had a huge trading network and some towns, such as Genoa and Venice in northern Italy, grew extremely wealthy importing and exporting goods, such as precious metals, silks, wool, and timber, either over land or by ship. In northern Europe, some trading towns including Lubeck, Hamburg, and Cologne, formed an alliance called the Hanseatic League to control trade. The league grew very powerful and, by 1400, had offices in 160 towns.

Did you know?

Venetian trader and explorer Marco Polo was one of the first westerners to travel along the Silk Road – the ancient overland trading route to China. He returned to Italy a wealthy man.

Camel caravan

Medieval trading towns

This map shows some of the main types of goods that were made in the different regions of medieval Europe. Use the information on the map and on page 13 to answer the questions below.

1. Name two things that might be sold by English merchants.

   ....

   ....

2. Which region produced mainly timber, furs, and rope?

   ....

3. What is the name of the overland trade route between eastern Europe and China?

   ....

4. What was the northern European trading alliance called?

   ....

5. Name three goods that were imported from the East, along the Silk Road.

   ....

   ....

   ....

6. How long might a big international trade fair last?

   ....

Coal   Amber   Wheat

Citrus fruit   Almonds   Armour   Cinnamon

Clothing

During the Middle Ages, people's clothes reflected their position in society. Rich nobles often wore exaggerated styles of clothing with elaborate headdresses, pointed shoes, and long, trailing garments trimmed with fur. Peasants wore simple clothes, suitable for working in the fields, including a woollen tunic, hose (leggings), and a linen shirt. Townspeople's clothes varied according to their status and wealth, with richer citizens wearing finely woven cloth and soft leather shoes or boots.

Clothing puzzle

These pictures show clothes worn by a medieval peasant and a townswoman. Number the parts of each picture to match the labels.

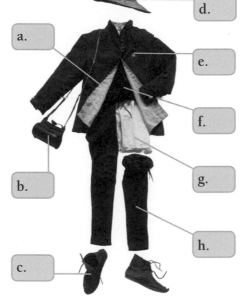

Townswoman
1. Woollen "kirtle" or dress
2. Leather purse that served as a pocket
3. Buckled leather shoes
4. Pin-on sleeve, worn on Sundays and special occasions
5. White linen shift, or undergarment
6. Linen head-wrap to keep hair hidden and clean
7. Wooden "patten" worn over shoes when muddy
8. Prayer beads

Peasant
1. Linen shirt
2. Blue woollen tunic fastened with laces, worn under a woollen jacket
3. Woollen jacket lined with linen
4. Hose (leggings) that could be rolled down when working in the fields
5. Leather working boots
6. Straw hat
7. Leather flask to carry ale
8. Cheap pewter good luck badge

Which headdress?

Number the three types of headdress worn by a rich noblewoman, according to their descriptions.

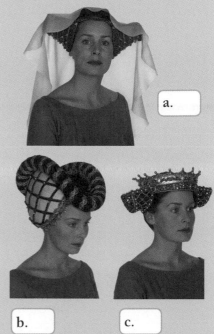

a.

b.   c.

1. Hair coiled under a horned headdress covered with a veil.
2. Coils of hair in curved "templers" above each ear.
3. Hair gathered in a hairnet, topped with a padded roll of fabric.

Did you know?

Wool to make clothes was often dyed with tree bark or the leaves and roots of plants.

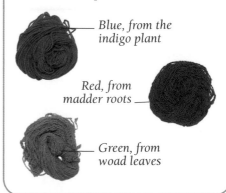

Blue, from the indigo plant

Red, from madder roots

Green, from woad leaves

Food and drink

In medieval times, rich people could afford to eat all kinds of food, including venison (deer), swans, dried fruits, almonds, and expensive spices. Ordinary people ate mainly coarse dark bread, garden vegetables, and meat such as pork or a trapped rabbit. Fish was served on Wednesdays, Fridays, and Saturdays, and during some Christian festivals, such as Lent. Most people ate salted or pickled herrings. The wealthy also enjoyed carp and pike from castle fishponds, or fresh river trout. The most common drinks were ale or wine.

Food quiz

Read the information on this page, then answer the questions below:

1. Name three herbs with which people flavoured their food.

....

2. What special name was given to vegetables used to thicken stews?

....

3. What was a thick broth called when it contained grains and meat stock? ....

4. Name one animal that provided "white meats"?................................

5. What was wastel?..

Cooking hearth puzzle

Number the following parts on this picture of a small stone hearth in a medieval manor.

1. Flat-bottomed iron pot

2. Metal ladle

3. Glazed earthenware cooking pot

4. Metal chain on which to hang pot over fire

5. Wood to burn as cooking fuel

6. Flue, for smoke to rise through thick castle wall

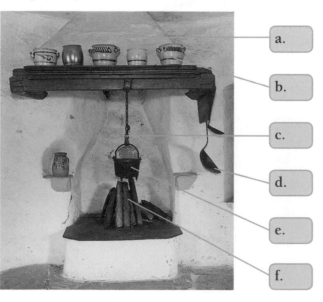

a.
b.
c.
d.
e.
f.

Did you know?

Most people ate wholewheat bread. Only the wealthy could afford to eat wastel – the finest bread made with white flour that had been sifted two or three times through a fine cloth.

Wholewheat brown bread

Cooking facts

- Most food was boiled in giant pots hung from hooks suspended over a fire, or roasted on spits.

- Food was flavoured with herbs, such as rosemary, parsley, and sage, and (for the wealthy) with spices such as nutmeg and cinnamon.

Rosemary **Parsley** **Sage**

- Vegetables such as turnips, leeks, onions, and cabbages were known as "pot-herbs", and were used to thicken soups and stews.

- Vegetables and grains (such as wheat, oats, or barley) were added to meat stock to make a thick broth called pottage.

- Milk from cows, sheep, and goats was used for cooking rather than drinking. Milk and other dairy foods were known as "white meats".

A medieval feast

Medieval banquets began late in the morning and lasted for several hours. A feast might include several courses of roasted meats and fish followed by sweet and spicy dishes. Most banquets included one or two subtleties – surprises such as a cooked bird with its head and feathers stuck back on, or a castle of marzipan. The lord's family and important guests sat at the high table at one end of the hall.

Feast menu

Find three stickers to decorate this menu for a king's banquet.

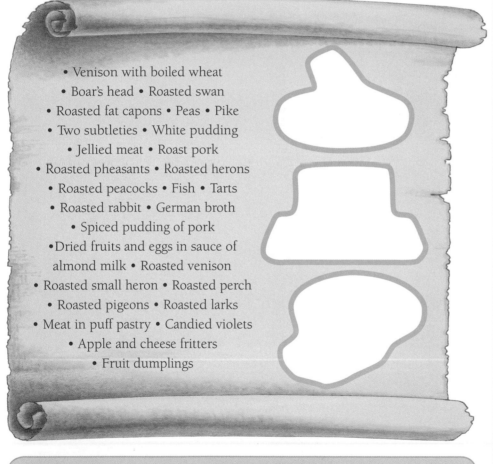

- Venison with boiled wheat
- Boar's head • Roasted swan
- Roasted fat capons • Peas • Pike
- Two subtleties • White pudding
- Jellied meat • Roast pork
- Roasted pheasants • Roasted herons
- Roasted peacocks • Fish • Tarts
- Roasted rabbit • German broth
- Spiced pudding of pork
- Dried fruits and eggs in sauce of almond milk • Roasted venison
- Roasted small heron • Roasted perch
- Roasted pigeons • Roasted larks
- Meat in puff pastry • Candied violets
- Apple and cheese fritters
- Fruit dumplings

Medieval food puzzle

Take a look at this list, then tick two things that people who lived during the Middle Ages did NOT eat. Use the menu above as a guide.

☐ Herons	☐ Peas	☐ Apples
☐ Cheese	☐ Violets	☐ Pineapples
☐ Potatoes	☐ Pigeon	☐ Pike

Did you know?

Instead of plates, food was served on thick slices of stale bread called trenchers, which soaked up gravy and grease.

Poor knights

Leftovers from a feast were usually given to the poor. This recipe (which is similar to French toast) was invented during the Middle Ages to use up stale bread. In many European countries the dish was known as "poor knights".

You will need:
- 2 slices of white bread
- 1 egg
- 1 teaspoon sugar
- 100 ml (3½ fl oz) milk
- ¼ teaspoon cinnamon or nutmeg
- Knob of butter
- Pinch of sugar and cinnamon

1 Beat the egg in a deep dish, then add the milk and sugar.

2 Dip the bread into the eggy mixture, until both sides are covered.

3 Heat the butter in a frying pan, and fry the bread until golden brown and the egg is cooked.

4 Sprinkle with a pinch of sugar and cinnamon.

 WARNING Ask an adult for help when frying the bread.

Fun and games

Medieval townspeople and peasants looked forward to holy days, or holidays, that marked important days in the Christian year, such as Christmas and Easter. Everyone took time off work to attend special church services and feasts. They might also be able to watch a mystery play, which told stories from the Bible, or be entertained by acrobats, jugglers, minstrels, mummers (masked actors), or even a dancing bear. Other festivals took place on Midsummer's Eve and at the bringing in of the harvest.

Did you know?

Most medieval people enjoyed gambling – even though it was frowned upon by the Church. People bet on dice games, wrestling matches, cockfights, and bear-baiting.

Pouch containing counters and dice

Play Fox and Geese

Here is how you can play Fox and Geese – a board game for two players enjoyed by people during the Middle Ages.

Copy the cross-shaped board onto a large sheet of cardboard. The board is made up of five large squares, divided into triangles. Cut 14 counters out of coloured card – 13 white geese and one red fox. Arrange the counters on the board, as shown.

How to play the game:

1 Decide who will be the fox and who will be the geese. The person who is the geese moves first.

2 Take it in turns to move, one counter each at a time. Each goose can only move forwards, either straight ahead or diagonally, to the next point on the board. The fox can move to the next point on the board in any direction.

3 If a goose is on the next adjacent point and there is a space behind it, the fox can jump over the goose to capture it. The captured goose remains out of play for the rest of the game.

4 The geese win if they hem in the fox so that it cannot move. The fox wins if he captures so many geese that the remaining geese are unable to hem him in.

Goose

Fox

Children playing Nine Men's Morris, another popular board game during the Middle Ages

Music and dancing

Most medieval people enjoyed playing and listening to music. In churches and cathedrals, monks and priests chanted texts in a beautiful form of singing known as plainchant, or plainsong. On feast days, people sang folk songs and danced to the sound of drums and pipes. By 1400, most medieval towns had their own town band of professional musicians who played drums, trumpets, and reed instruments called shawms.

Did you know?

Music was first written down in medieval times. Choirmasters in monasteries wrote musical signs above the words in prayer books, to help them remember the rise and fall of the music.

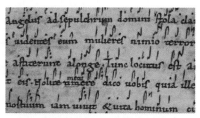

Early music notation

Musical instruments

Find five stickers to complete this table showing medieval musical instruments and how they were played.

Shawm – a reed instrument played by blowing down it, while covering holes with the fingers

Nakers – small drums hung in pairs on a belt and beaten with short sticks, often to accompany dancers

Lute – played by strumming or plucking the strings with one hand, while pressing the strings with the other to change the notes.

Bagpipes – a wind instrument played by blowing down a mouthpiece to inflate a bag, and covering the pipe's holes with the fingertips

Pipe and tabor – a three-holed pipe held in one hand, and a drum with a "snare" (a tight string to add a buzzing sound) played with the other hand

Dance facts

- Dance music was usually provided by drums and pipes.
- Some dances, such as the pavan, were slow, with couples dancing side by side in a procession.
- Other dances, such as the piva and saltarello, were lively and quick with lots of spins, hops, and turns.
- The estampida was a slow, courtly dance. It was probably danced by couples and included sliding steps and the stamping of feet.
- From the 13th century, people created a new dance called the *danse macabre* or dance of death. This dance usually took place in cemeteries or holy places, with dancers led by someone dressed as a skeleton.

Medieval dancers

Music quiz

Circle the correct words in the following sentences using the information on this page to help you.

1. Small drums were called **shawms / nakers / lutes**.
2. The **saltarello / pavan / tabor** was a slow, processional dance.
3. Medieval monks sang **folk songs / plainsong / saltarellos**.
4. The **bagpipes / shawm / lute** was a stringed instrument.
5. A quick, lively dance was the **piva / pavan / pipe and tabor**.

Medieval cathedrals

In the 12th century, a new Gothic style of architecture appeared in which heavy stone-tiled roofs were held up by huge stone frameworks, which had spaces, or vaults, in their ribbed ceilings to make them lighter, and huge buttresses to support their soaring walls. This allowed builders to pierce the walls with tall arched windows. The windows were then filled with panels of bright stained glass, flooding the interiors with light.

Label the cathedral

This picture shows the Gothic cathedral of Notre Dame in Paris, France. Work started on the cathedral in 1163 and it took 200 years to complete. Name the parts of the cathedral using the descriptions in the box below.

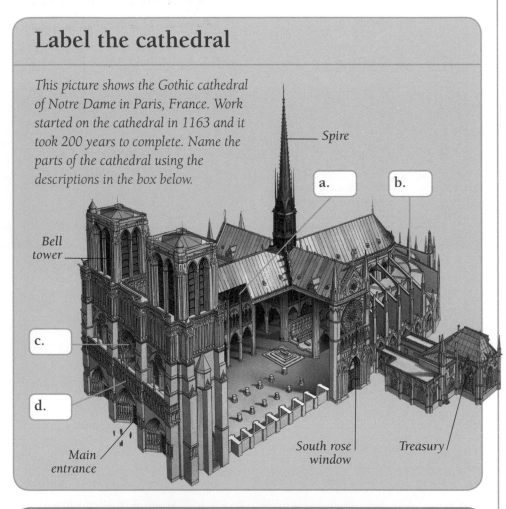

Spire

a.

b.

Bell tower

c.

d.

Main entrance

South rose window

Treasury

Cathedral facts

1. **Rose window** A circular stained glass window above the main entrance.

2. **The King's gallery** A row of 28 carved stone statues of kings, above the main entrance.

3. **Flying buttress** An arched support holding up the walls at the eastern end of the cathedral.

4. **Pointed arched window** Gothic-style window with delicate carved stone supports.

Design a window

Follow these steps to make your own stained-glass window. You will need black cardboard, a translucent coloured substance that lets light shine through (such as sweet wrappers or cellophane), a craft knife or scissors, and glue.

! WARNING Ask an adult for help when using a craft knife.

Finished window

1 Sketch your design lightly on a sheet of black cardboard. Divide up your picture into small parts. Try to keep the lines separating each part of the picture wide and even.

2 Carefully cut out the shapes where you are going to glue your coloured paper.

3 Glue pieces of translucent paper over each of the spaces in your design.

4 Hang your design in a window, so the light shines through.

Living in a monastery

Medieval religious houses included monasteries and abbeys ruled by abbots, nunneries or convents ruled by abbesses, and priories ruled by a prior. The heart of every monastery was its church, where the monks gathered to worship at set times each day. In between prayers, monks worked in the garden, tended livestock, decorated manuscripts, or looked after the sick.

Did you know?

Church services were in Latin, the language of ancient Rome. Some of the monks' jobs had Latin names. For example, "cantor" is Latin for singer.

Label the monastery

This picture shows a model of a monastery. Read the descriptions below, then find and number each part of the monastery in the picture.

1. Monks slept in the **dorter**, or dormitory, which contained rows of beds.
2. Vegetables and herbs grew in the **garden**.
3. The monks ate at long tables in the **refectory**.
4. The **infirmary**, or hospital, was in a separate building near the gatehouse, to reduce the risk of spreading infection.
5. The **cloister** was a covered walkway surrounding a courtyard.
6. Monks met to discuss monastery business in the **chapterhouse** next to the church.

Church

Gatehouse

a.
b.
c.
d.
e.
f.

Match the monks

Look at these names for the different monks living in an abbey. Using the information on this page and on page 11, draw lines to match the monks to their job descriptions.

1. Abbot
2. Almoner
3. Barber surgeon
4. Infirmarian
5. Lector
6. Cantor
7. Cellarer

a. Shaved the monks' faces and tonsures and performed some surgery.
b. Led the singing in the abbey's choir.
c. Looked after the cellars where the abbey's provisions were stored.
d. Dispensed alms to the sick and the poor.
e. Looked after the infirmary.
f. Was in charge of the whole abbey.
g. Read from the bible in church or in the refectory during mealtimes, resting his book on a lectern.

Monk's medicine jug

The written word

Books were rare during the Middle Ages because they were handwritten, mainly by monks working in their monastery's scriptorium. After 1200, books became more common as professional scribes and illuminators began to earn a living making copies of books for wealthy customers. One of the most popular types of book ordered by nobles was a personal book of psalms called a psalter.

Illuminating puzzle

These captions explain how a capital letter is illuminated in gold leaf. Number the captions from 1 to 4 to put them in the correct order, then find two stickers to complete the sequence.

a. The gold leaf is rubbed, or burnished, with a traditional burnishing tool, such as a dog's or wolf's tooth attached to a wooden handle.

b. Gesso, a kind of sticky glue often made from plaster, lead, water, sugar, and egg white, is applied to the illuminator's design with a goose quill.

c. The illuminator finally paints the rest of the background around the gilding. As long as it has been well burnished, the gold will remain shiny.

d. The gesso is left to set. The illuminator presses a sheet of gold leaf firmly over the gesso and removes the surplus gold with a soft brush.

Mix-and-match writers

Draw lines to match each writer to the correct description. Use the information on your back-cover chart to help you.

1. **Chaucer**
2. **Dante**
3. **Boccaccio**
4. **Petrarch**

a. Italian writer, famous for *The Divine Comedy*, a journey through Hell and Purgatory to Paradise.

b. English author of *The Canterbury Tales*.

c. Italian scholar, famous for his love poetry and songs.

d. Italian author of *The Decameron*, the first European book written in a realistic, narrative story style.

A medieval bookshop

Disease and death

Many people living in the Middle Ages did not survive much beyond their 30th birthday. People died in wars and through famine (starvation) and disease. Medical knowledge was limited, and people believed they could be cured through spells, prayers, or making a pilgrimage to a holy place. The Black Death, carried by black rats on ships returning to Europe from Asia, was a deadly, contagious plague. Between 1347 and 1350, it killed around one-third of the entire population of Europe.

Herbal medicine

Find four stickers to complete this chart of common herbs used to treat patients during the Middle Ages.

Lungwort was used to treat chest disorders.	**Marjoram** was used to reduce bruising and swelling.	**Feverfew** was used to treat headaches.	**Lemon balm** was used to cure fevers and colds.	**Wormwood** was used to cure stomach ache.

Medicine quiz

Use the information on this page to answer the following questions.

1. What was a "simple"?...

2. What was lemon balm thought to cure?...

3. What herb might be given to someone with stomach ache?...................
....

4. Name the four humours of the body...
....

5. Which humour do you think might be thought to be out of balance for a doctor to prescribe blood-letting? ....

6. What was the Black Death?..

Medicine facts

- People believed that everyone had four humours relating to the elements – black bile (earth), phlegm (water), blood (air), and yellow bile (fire). It was thought that people became sick if their humours were out of balance.

- Physicians and apothecaries (a medieval town's modern-day pharmacist) examined the patient's blood, urine, and stools, then prescribed herbs or medicines to restore the body's balance of humours.

- Herbal remedies called simples were common. Patients took herbs raw or stewed in hot water, like tea.

- Other treatments included taking a hot bath, eating ground earthworms or animal dung, and releasing blood by cutting a patient's vein (blood-letting) or using leeches.

Medieval apothecary and his patient

Did you know?

Medieval doctors were sometimes called "leeches" because they tried to cure patients by using leeches to suck their blood.

History of the Middle Ages

Tick or number the boxes to answer each question. Check your answers on page 46.

1 The early part of the Middle Ages is called the:

☐ **a.** Renaissance
☐ **b.** Dark Ages
☐ **c.** High Middle Ages
☐ **d.** Age of Discovery

2 The Benedictine order of monks was founded around the year:

☐ **a.** 500
☐ **b.** 750
☐ **c.** 1000
☐ **d.** 1500

3 In which year did William of Normany conquer England?

☐ **a.** 666
☐ **b.** 1066
☐ **c.** 1266
☐ **d.** 1366

4 The French king who fought in the Crusades and was made into a saint was called:

☐ **a.** Henry II
☐ **b.** Louis IX
☐ **c.** Otto the Great
☐ **d.** Charlemagne

5 The Black Death swept across Europe in the:

☐ **a.** 1100s
☐ **b.** 1200s
☐ **c.** 1300s
☐ **d.** 1400s

6 The Hundred Years' War between France and England began in:

☐ **a.** 1117
☐ **b.** 1227
☐ **c.** 1337
☐ **d.** 1447

7 Who was king of England in 1415?

☐ **a.** Alfred the Great
☐ **b.** Henry V
☐ **c.** Richard III
☐ **d.** William the Conqueror (William I)

8 Who printed an early version of the Bible on his printing press in 1455?

☐ **a.** Dante
☐ **b.** Gutenberg
☐ **c.** Giotto
☐ **d.** Boccaccio

9 Number these events 1 to 5, in the order in which they happened.

☐ **a.** The Crusades began.
☐ **b.** The Black Death swept across Europe.
☐ **c.** Christopher Columbus discovered the "New World".
☐ **d.** King John of England was forced to accept the Magna Carta.

10 Which empire was destroyed by the Ottoman Turks in 1453?

☐ **a.** Roman
☐ **b.** British
☐ **c.** Holy Roman
☐ **d.** Byzantine

Medieval society

Tick or number the boxes to answer each question. Check your answers on page 46.

1 The feudal system was introduced into England by:

☐ **a.** Alfred the Great
☐ **b.** the Normans
☐ **c.** Charlemagne
☐ **d.** the Vikings

2 In the feudal system, which people had the fewest rights?

☐ **a.** Barons
☐ **b.** Peasants
☐ **c.** Bishops
☐ **d.** Knights

3 Medieval kings usually governed their kingdom through a:

☐ **a.** Great Council
☐ **b.** Great Diocese
☐ **c.** Great Gathering
☐ **d.** Great Charter

4 A fief was:

☐ **a.** land given in return for services
☐ **b.** a knight, sworn to serve his lord
☐ **c.** a tax paid to the Church
☐ **d.** a servant on a manor

5 A person bound by oath to serve his lord was called a:

☐ **a.** scutage
☐ **b.** fief
☐ **c.** vassal
☐ **d.** reeve

6 Which of the following facts about peasants is not true?

☐ **a.** Peasants belonged to their lord.
☐ **b.** They were not allowed to leave the manor without permission.
☐ **c.** They could never become free.
☐ **d.** They had to give their lord grain to use his mill.
☐ **e.** They could read and write.

7 What was the life expectancy of a European peasant during the Middle Ages?

☐ **a.** 15 years
☐ **b.** 25 years
☐ **c.** 35 years
☐ **d.** 45 years

8 Which of the following did a noblewoman usually not do while her husband was away?

☐ **a.** run the estate
☐ **b.** work in the fields
☐ **c.** settle local disputes
☐ **d.** look after the money
☐ **e.** spin wool into thread

9 "Shield money" or scutage was:

☐ **a.** money paid not to fight
☐ **b.** the price of buying a jousting shield
☐ **c.** a fee for buying a coat-of-arms
☐ **d.** a tax paid to the Church

10 What sort of entertainment was found at court?

☐ **a.** jousts
☐ **b.** tourneys
☐ **c.** dancing
☐ **d.** gambling
☐ **e.** board games
☐ **f.** music

11 Which was not a typical medieval punishment?

☐ **a.** being whipped
☐ **b.** being put in the stocks
☐ **c.** being shot
☐ **d.** being put in a pillory
☐ **e.** being hanged

Medieval warriors

Tick or number the boxes to answer each question. Check your answers on page 46.

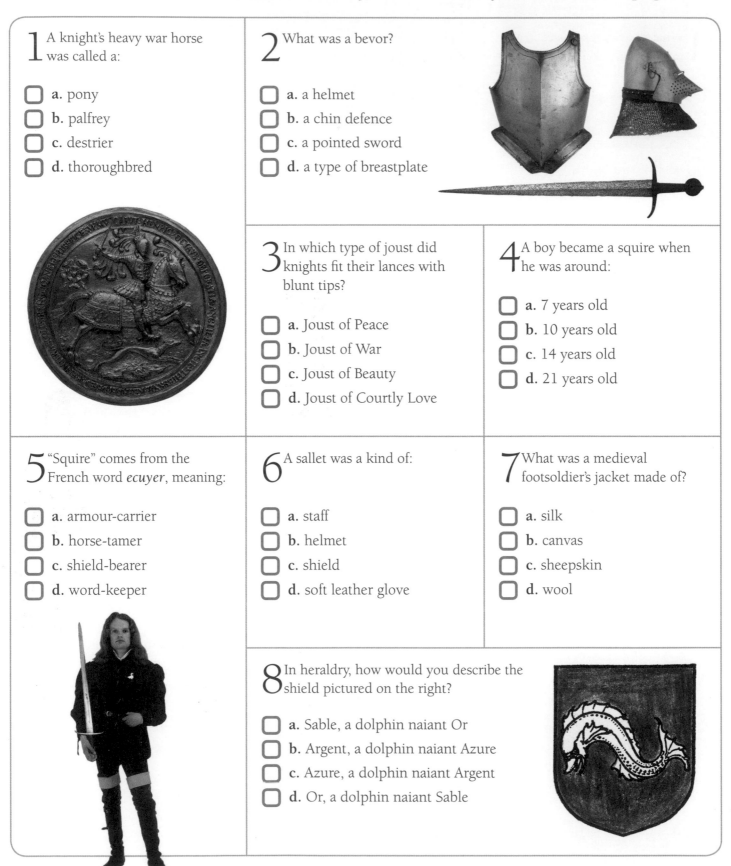

1 A knight's heavy war horse was called a:

- a. pony
- b. palfrey
- c. destrier
- d. thoroughbred

2 What was a bevor?

- a. a helmet
- b. a chin defence
- c. a pointed sword
- d. a type of breastplate

3 In which type of joust did knights fit their lances with blunt tips?

- a. Joust of Peace
- b. Joust of War
- c. Joust of Beauty
- d. Joust of Courtly Love

4 A boy became a squire when he was around:

- a. 7 years old
- b. 10 years old
- c. 14 years old
- d. 21 years old

5 "Squire" comes from the French word *ecuyer*, meaning:

- a. armour-carrier
- b. horse-tamer
- c. shield-bearer
- d. word-keeper

6 A sallet was a kind of:

- a. staff
- b. helmet
- c. shield
- d. soft leather glove

7 What was a medieval footsoldier's jacket made of?

- a. silk
- b. canvas
- c. sheepskin
- d. wool

8 In heraldry, how would you describe the shield pictured on the right?

- a. Sable, a dolphin naiant Or
- b. Argent, a dolphin naiant Azure
- c. Azure, a dolphin naiant Argent
- d. Or, a dolphin naiant Sable

Daily life

Tick or number the boxes to answer each question. Check your answers on page 46.

1 What did not take place in a castle's great hall?

☐ **a.** dancing
☐ **b.** sleeping
☐ **c.** feasting
☐ **d.** conducting business
☐ **e.** making armour

2 Which person did not work on a medieval manor?

☐ **a.** bailiff
☐ **b.** reeve
☐ **c.** abbot
☐ **d.** steward

3 In which season would peasants usually pick fruit, nuts, and berries?

☐ **a.** spring
☐ **b.** summer
☐ **c.** autumn
☐ **d.** winter

4 Which of the following was not a medieval musical instrument?

☐ **a.** a tabor
☐ **b.** a psaltery
☐ **c.** a lute
☐ **d.** a shawm

5 A mummer was a:

☐ **a.** type of dance
☐ **b.** musical instrument
☐ **c.** masked actor
☐ **d.** herbal cure

6 What was a psalter?

☐ **a.** a salt cellar
☐ **b.** a prayer book
☐ **c.** a pot-herb
☐ **d.** a type of clothing

7 What was "white meat"?

☐ **a.** a type of dairy food
☐ **b.** fine white bread
☐ **c.** a pot-herb
☐ **d.** a thick broth

8 Which two foods did everyone eat during the Middle Ages?

☐ **a.** pottage
☐ **b.** wild boar
☐ **c.** venison
☐ **d.** bread

9 A kirtle was a:

☐ **a.** soft felt hat
☐ **b.** woollen dress
☐ **c.** long shirt
☐ **d.** pin-on sleeve

10 What might be worn over shoes to protect them from mud?

☐ **a.** puddles
☐ **b.** pattens
☐ **c.** patterns
☐ **d.** pitchers

11 What was a "simple"?

☐ **a.** an easy way of blood-letting
☐ **b.** a type of "cure-all"
☐ **c.** a herbal remedy
☐ **d.** a potion of ground earthworms

Guilds and trades

Tick or number the boxes to answer each question. Check your answers on page 46.

1 Where might a medieval town develop?

- [ ] **a.** by a castle
- [ ] **b.** around a crossroads
- [ ] **c.** near a rivermouth
- [ ] **d.** by a natural harbour

2 Townspeople had the right to govern themselves through a:

- [ ] **a.** charter
- [ ] **b.** burgess
- [ ] **c.** council
- [ ] **d.** curfew

3 A burgess was a:

- [ ] **a.** town charter
- [ ] **b.** free citizen
- [ ] **c.** town market
- [ ] **d.** lord's domain

4 Which of the following might be found in a typical medieval town?

- [ ] **a.** stone walls
- [ ] **b.** gatehouses
- [ ] **c.** public bathhouses
- [ ] **d.** workshops

5 Town markets were usually held:

- [ ] **a.** every day
- [ ] **b.** two or three times a week
- [ ] **c.** once a month
- [ ] **d.** twice a year

6 Medieval associations of craftspeople were called:

- [ ] **a.** burgesses
- [ ] **b.** guilds
- [ ] **c.** schools
- [ ] **d.** chambers

7 Put these stages in learning a trade in order, starting with the earliest.

- [ ] **a.** joins a guild
- [ ] **b.** becomes a journeyman
- [ ] **c.** becomes an apprentice
- [ ] **d.** takes on an apprentice

8 Which of the following goods came mainly from the Baltic?

- [ ] **a.** coal and metalwork
- [ ] **b.** amber and goose feathers
- [ ] **c.** spices and jewels
- [ ] **d.** brocade cloth

9 Banking began in

- [ ] **a.** England
- [ ] **b.** Italy
- [ ] **c.** France
- [ ] **d.** Germany

10 The golden florin was minted in Florence in

- [ ] **a.** 1352
- [ ] **b.** 1252
- [ ] **c.** 1152
- [ ] **d.** 1052

The medieval Church

Tick or number the boxes to answer each question. Check your answers on page 46.

1 The Church's lands were organised into:

☐ **a.** fiefs
☐ **b.** dioceses
☐ **c.** councils
☐ **d.** duchies

2 What was a pointed bishop's hat called?

☐ **a.** archbishop
☐ **b.** psaltery
☐ **c.** crozier
☐ **d.** mitre

3 What were Church taxes called?

☐ **a.** tides
☐ **b.** tallies
☐ **c.** tithes
☐ **d.** titles

4 How much did peasants have to give of what they produced to the Church?

☐ **a.** one-half
☐ **b.** one-quarter
☐ **c.** one-tenth
☐ **d.** one-third

5 What might a parish priest NOT be able to do?

☐ **a.** collect tithes
☐ **b.** marry people
☐ **c.** christen babies
☐ **d.** rule a diocese
☐ **e.** look after the poor

6 What might be found in a medieval cathedral?

☐ **a.** stained-glass windows
☐ **b.** wooden carvings
☐ **c.** painted panels
☐ **d.** stone statues
☐ **e.** flying buttresses

7 The first monastic order was founded by:

☐ **a.** St Peter
☐ **b.** St Benedict
☐ **c.** St Francis
☐ **d.** St Thomas Aquinas

8 Monasteries were usually ruled by:

☐ **a.** bishops
☐ **b.** priests
☐ **c.** abbots
☐ **d.** archbishops

9 In which room of a monastery did monks eat?

☐ **a.** dorter
☐ **b.** refectory
☐ **c.** chapterhouse
☐ **d.** cloister

10 Which of the following jobs was NOT done in a typical medieval monastery?

☐ **a.** growing vegetables
☐ **b.** copying religious manuscripts
☐ **c.** training for war
☐ **d.** looking after sick people
☐ **e.** making wine and ale

11 Who was the head of the Catholic Church?

☐ **a.** the King
☐ **b.** the Pope
☐ **c.** the Archbishop of Canterbury
☐ **d.** the Holy Roman Emperor

Activity answers

Once you have completed each page of activities, check your answers below.

Pages 14–15
Finish the timeline
476	Last Roman Emperor in the West loses power
768	Charlemagne becomes ruler
962	Otto the Great is crowned
1066	Battle of Hastings
1210	Francis of Assisi
c. 1267	Giotto is born
1346	Battle of Crécy
c. 1386	The Canterbury Tales
1415	Battle of Agincourt
1492	Christopher Columbus crosses the Atlantic

Page 15
Name it!

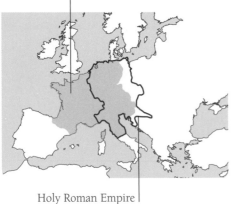

Charlemagne's empire

Holy Roman Empire

Page 16
Name it!
1 psaltery
2 floor tile
3 folding book
4 belt buckle
5 chamber pot
6 calendar stave

Page 17
Who's who in the feudal system
1 king
  nobles
2 bishops
  barons
3 knights
4 peasants

Feudal word puzzle
1 b
2 d
3 c
4 a

Page 18
Castle quiz
a	3	h	12
b	1	i	9
c	2	j	6
d	5	k	11
e	8	l	13
f	4	m	7
g	10	n	14

Page 19
Building a castle
1	c	4	b
2	f	5	d
3	a	6	e

Castle history
a	2	Stone keep
b	3	Concentric castle
c	1	Motte and bailey castle

Page 20
Mix-and-match kings
1	c	4	a
2	b	5	f
3	d	6	e

Page 20
King and court life quiz
1 Two of the following: tournaments, jousts, and minstrels making music
2 Chivalry
3 *cheval* (horse)
4 Courtly love

Page 21
Arming a knight
a	2	d	1
b	5	e	6
c	3	f	4

Making a knight
1 page
2 squire
3 armour, horses
4 21

Page 22
Joust quiz
1 to train for battle, or war
2 tourneys, or mêlées
3 jousts of war
4 tilt barrier
5 crown-shaped lance tip (to make the lance blunt)

Joust puzzle

Cloth pavilions

Banner

Knight on horseback

Raised box

The list

Jousting knights

Wounded knight

Page 23
Match the shield
a	3	e	7
b	4	f	6
c	5	g	1
d	2	h	8

Page 24
On the march
A novel and a printed map would NOT be carried in a medieval soldier's pack.

Ready for war
1 canvas
2 arms and hands
3 buckler
4 head
5 staff weapon

Page 25
Jobs on the manor
1 d   4 a
2 b   5 c
3 e

Hunting puzzle
a servants
b wild boar
c lord
d tracker
e huntsman
f deer

Page 26
The farming year
1 winter
2 summer
3 spring
4 autumn

How much tax?
The peasant would need to give the priest:
    1 sack of wheat grain
    3 bundles of firewood
    65 eggs
    $\frac{1}{10}$th of a barrel of ale

Page 27
Learning a trade
a 4
b 2
c 1
d 3

Page 27
True or false?
1 True   4 True
2 False   5 False
3 True

Page 28
Medieval trading towns
1 coal, wool, or tin
2 Scandinavia
3 the Silk Road
4 Hanseatic League
5 spices, perfume, silk, or jewels
6 two weeks

Page 29
Clothing puzzle
Townswoman:	Peasant:
a 6	a 3
b 8	b 7
c 2	c 5
d 3	d 6
e 5	e 8
f 4	f 2
g 1	g 1
h 7	h 4

Which headdress?
a 1
b 3
c 2

Page 30
Food quiz
1 rosemary, parsley, and sage
2 pot-herbs
3 pottage
4 one of: cows, sheep, goats
5 fine, white bread made from sieved flour (eaten by the wealthy)

Cooking hearth puzzle
a 6   d 2
b 3   e 1
c 4   f 5

Page 31
Medieval food puzzle
Potatoes, pineapples – these were later brought from the New World

Page 33
Music quiz
1 nakers
2 pavan
3 plainsong
4 lute
5 piva

Page 34
Label the cathedral
a 4
b 3
c 1
d 2

Page 35
Label the monastery
a 6   d 2
b 5   e 4
c 3   f 1

Match the monks
1 f   5 g
2 d   6 b
3 a   7 c
4 e

Page 36
Illuminating puzzle
a 3
b 1
c 4
d 2

Mix-and-match writers
1 b
2 a
3 d
4 c

Page 37
Medicine quiz
1 a herbal remedy
2 fevers and colds
3 wormwood
4 black bile/earth, phlegm/water, blood/air, yellow bile/fire
5 blood (air)
6 a deadly disease; the plague

Quick quiz answers

Once you have completed each page of quiz questions, check your answers below.

page 38
History of the Middle Ages
1 b 2 a 3 b 4 b 5 c 6 c 7 b 8 b
9 a1, b3, c4, d2 10 d

page 39
Medieval society
1 b 2 b 3 a 4 a 5 c 6 c e 7 b
8 b 9 a 10 a b c d e f 11 c

page 40
Medieval warriors
1 c 2 b 3 a 4 c 5 c 6 b 7 b 8 c

page 41
Daily life
1 e 2 c 3 c 4 b 5 c 6 b 7 a 8 a d
9 b 10 b 11 c

page 42
Guilds and trades
1 a b c d 2 a 3 b 4 a b c d 5 b 6 b
7 a3, b2, c1, d4 8 b 9 b 10 b

page 43
The medieval church
1 b 2 d 3 c 4 c 5 d 6 a b c d e
7 b 8 c 9 b 10 c 11 b

Acknowledgements

The publisher would like to thank the following:

Susan McKeever for assessing the manuscript; Monica Byles for proof-reading.

The publisher would like to thank the following for their kind permission to reproduce their photographs:

Key: a-above; b-below/bottom; c-centre; f-far; l-left; r-right; t-top

DK Images: Ashmolean Museum, Oxford 17c; The British Library 3cr, 15c, 16ca, 33tr, 36br, 43bc; Chateau de Saumur 16cla; Danish National Museum 16c; Anthony Barton Collection 16fcla; British Museum 10cl, 20;

Musee de Cluny 26tr; Musee des Thermes et de l'Hotel de Cluny, Paris 26bc; Musee National du Moyen-Age Thermes de Cluny 27crb; Museum of the Order of St John, London 23tr, 35br; Stephen Oliver 10cr; The Order of the Black Prince 7br; Saxon Village Crafts, Battle, East Sussex 36tr; Universitets Oldsaksamling, Oslo 6bl; By kind permission of the Trustees of the Wallace Collection 7cl, 16cl, 17crb, 29br, 39c, 40tr; Weald and Downland Open Air Museum 12cr.

Stickers: DK Images: Anthony Barton Collection 1cb, 1cla, 2clb, 2tr; The British Library 2c; British Museum 1clb, 1tr, 2tl; Museum of English Rural Life, The University of Reading 1crb; By kind permission of the Trustees of the Wallace Collection 1cr, 2cr.

Jacket: Front: DK Images: Anthony Barton Collection clb (lute). Back: DK Images: Wallace Collection, London bl. Back flap: DK Images: Bayerische Verwaltung der Staatlichen Schlosser, Garten und Seen tl; The British Library bl; Rough Guides tr; Wallace Collection, London bl; Jerry Young cra; NASA: cl.

All other images © Dorling Kindersley
For further information see:
www.dkimages.com

PROGRESS CHART

Chart your progress as you work through the activity and quiz pages in this book.
First check your answers, then stick a gold star in the correct box below.

Page	Topic	Star	Page	Topic	Star	Page	Topic	Star
14	Medieval timeline	⭐	24	A soldier's life	⭐	34	Medieval cathedrals	⭐
15	Medieval timeline	⭐	25	Living on a manor	⭐	35	Living in a monastery	⭐
16	Medieval remains	⭐	26	A peasant's lot	⭐	36	The written word	⭐
17	A feudal society	⭐	27	Town life	⭐	37	Disease and death	⭐
18	Castle life	⭐	28	Trade across Europe	⭐	38	History of the Middle Ages	⭐
19	Castle life	⭐	29	Clothing	⭐	39	Medieval society	⭐
20	Court and kings	⭐	30	Food and drink	⭐	40	Medieval warriors	⭐
21	Medieval knights	⭐	31	A medieval feast	⭐	41	Daily life	⭐
22	Training for battle	⭐	32	Fun and games	⭐	42	Guilds and trades	⭐
23	Heraldry for battle	⭐	33	Music and dancing	⭐	43	The medieval Church	⭐

EYEWITNESS PROJECT BOOKS
MEDIEVAL LIFE

★ ★ ★ ★ ★ ★ ★ ★

CERTIFICATE OF EXCELLENCE

Congratulations to

(Name) ....

for successfully completing this book on

(Award date) ....